THE BAKER'S DOZEN
Cookbook Series Volume 2

BEST BISCOTTI

EXTRA! FREE BONUS! 4 MONTH SUBSCRIPTION TO BETTERBAKING.COM

BESTSELLING AUTHOR OF TREASURY OF JEWISH HOLIDAY BAKING

Marcy Goldman

Creator, Betterbaking.com

The Baker's Dozen Cookbook Series

Volume 2

Best Biscotti

Marcy Goldman

River Heart Press
Montreal, Canada

The Baker's Dozen Series, Volume Two
Marcy Goldman Presents: The Baker's Dozen Best Biscotti
Text and Recipes by Marcy Goldman

River Heart Press
Montreal, Canada

Marcy Goldman is a cookbook author, master baker and host of the www.BetterBaking.com and www.MarcyGoldman.com. Inquiries may be sent to editors@betterbaking.com

Photographs by Marcy Goldman, Ryan Szulc, Flicker, Shutterstock, Big Stock Photo

Library and Archives Canada in Publication
ISBN 978-1-927936-25-2 Print Book
ISBN 978-1-927936-19-1 Ebook

Goldman, Marcy
The Baker's Dozen Series, Volume Two
Marcy Goldman Presents: The Baker's Dozen Best Biscotti

Other Books by Marcy Goldman
Marcy Goldman is a cookbook author, master baker and host of www.Betterbaking.com and www.MarcyGoldman.com. Her publishing imprint is River Heart Press, Montreal, Canada. In addition, she has published with Random House U.S. and Canada, Doubleday, Broadway Books, Ten Speed Press and Oxmoor House. Inquires may be sent to marcygoldman01@gmail.com or via www.Betterbaking.com.

Best Holiday Cookies, The Baker's Dozen, Volume One 2017 River Heart Press Print
The 10th Anniversary Edition of Treasury of Jewish Holiday Baking, 2017 River Heart Press
The Baker's Four Seasons 2014, River Heart Press
A Passion for Baking, 2014 River Heart Press
Love and Ordinary Things, 2014 River Heart Press
When Bakers Cook, 2013 River Heart Press
A Treasury of Jewish Holiday Baking, 2007
The New Best of Betterbaking.com, 2007 Whitecap Books

Library and Archives Canada Cataloguing in Publication

Goldman, Marcy

Baking 2. Biscotti
1 Title

Contents

The Baker's Dozen Cookbook Series

Volume Two
Best Biscotti

Welcome to The Baker's Dozen Thirteen Best Biscotti cookbook! This is the second volume in my Baker's Dozen thirteen book series, each volume devoted to very special collection of my own original recipes of blue-ribbon winners. Each book in the series is a baker's dozen (thirteen recipes) of one special genre of baking. In this case, it's the baker's dozen of best biscotti.

How The Baker's Dozen Series was Born

A few years ago, when I first began publishing my own cookbooks alongside my cookbook career in traditional publishing with large publishing houses, I looked at the cookbook publishing landscape and wealth of free recipes online. Given all these free recipes and changes in how readers find and enjoy recipes, I had to ask: "*What do people really want in a cookbook?*" I also have two decades of being at the helm of my own website, www.Betterbaking.com to draw some conclusions from. I know my readers and their baking habits and along with my own preferences of a baker, I have a hunch what people are looking for when they research recipes they want to make.

I know people like recipes that are fast, easy and reward with excellent results! People also prefer recipes that are 100% tested by the creator and a team of capable, experienced baking testers. That's when the notion for a series of e-cookbooks, each specializing in one baking subject, popped into my head. Why not make one little book with thirteen (a baker's dozen) of the best of my best?

Most of my previous cookbooks have been huge affairs of over 200 recipes per book! But I like the idea (as a reader and a baker/cook myself) of focussing on *one genre* of baking that celebrates the best of a particular kind of baking. That way, it's not too much or too little. When you add thirteen best baking tips along with thirteen best recipes, you have (or so I think!) a pretty nice and natural concept.

As a master baker, I've long wanted to share my best biscotti recipes in just such a perfect little book along with all my baker's tricks of the trade and you'll only find the best of my best so you can bake your best – which is what my mission at www.Betterbaking.com has always been about.

Where does the phrase 'a baker's dozen' originate?

According to UrbanDictionary.com it goes something like this:

In the Medieval Ages there was a period when bakers began cheating the public at such a rate that public outcry reached the ears of several kings. As bread was a daily staple of medieval life, the bakers knew that they could charge a lot of money for minimal portions of their products. As such, kings levied laws against bakers stating that they were to lower their prices and keep honest. The term "A Baker's Dozen" (meaning 13 instead of 12) came from this time period. Any baker caught selling less than an even dozen was strictly and harshly punished. As a result bakers began adding one extra loaf, bun or cookie (for a total of thirteen units, versus 12 units of whatever it was) just to be certain their count would be correct or even over the amount decreed by law.

If that isn't a case for being generous, I don't know what is. These days, a *baker's dozen* is a generic term that has simply come to mean an extra or one bonus anything. In this case, it refers to this 13-recipe book concept for a series of mini cookbooks.

A Baker's Dozen Recipe Collection and A Baker's Dozen Secret Baking Tips

My emphasis in this little premier baker's dozen cookbook has been to create both definitive classic cookies as well as some that are decidedly more global in their roots. Each is innately elegant and uplifts the cookie paradigm. I created each recipe to be a pearl in your baking repertoire. Each recipe has been tested over four times by one of my wonderful baking test volunteers (you'll see their names in the Acknowledgements)

In order for you to bake your best of my best, I've also tucked thirteen, secret baker's tips for each of the recipes. These are my best tricks as a professional baker and pastry chef that I am delighted to share with you. It's to offer further insurance for your baking success and bestow you with extra baking confidence (and knowledge – even if you're a pro yourself). Each and any one of these tips has the power to boost your baking by a quantum leap.

B is for Biscotti

Some bakery trends come and go but others innately founded on a more enduring premise, become classic. There has to be a lasting appeal and biscotti fits the bill. Biscotti, a lovely, crisp, crunchy, sophisticated cookie are also elegant, versatile, infinitely dunkable and munchable. No wonder biscotti hits all the right notes; it has *everything* going for it.

Biscotti in the 90's in North American seemed to rise with the gourmet coffee trend (thank you Starbucks). These days, slick and well-marketed biscotti companies sprout up almost every other day, each with their own signature. There are also the toney glass canisters that display biscotti which is as much a fixture in the cafe-bars as those gorgeous espresso machines. There are also commercial biscotti, all presumably conceived on "Mama's" or "Nona's" secret, generations-old recipe or start-up baking companies who package their goods in pretty bags or boxes. (Of course, you don't need to be a coffee consumer to love biscotti; tea lovers adore biscotti just as much)

Bigger, more decadent desserts are fine for some and special occasions, especially for a crowd but biscotti are perfect when you just want to quietly celebrate one of those smaller (and just as precious) moments of your life – a friend drops by, you have an hour and a good book to yourself or you want to bring in something to treat the office crew and brighten their day. Biscotti are just perfect!

Biscotti are an indelible part of the Italian kitchen, although recipes vary from region to region. Italian friends confide that rather than restrict it to a coffee break treat as we do here, biscotti, also known as *cantuccini* (although that terms really references almond biscotti), is just as often a breakfast staple, eaten with the first coffee of the day. Heritage Italian biscotti, compared to the North American spin on things, are innately rustic and satisfying. I myself like both biscotti plain or with frills (nuts and chocolate) but all biscotti somehow has something in it that makes it special.

What makes biscotti unique as a cookie is that it is "twice baked", (hence the preface "bis", meaning "again" as in "baked again or baked twice"), once in a log shape, and the second time, cut in slices, to dry and crisp the dough into crisp, lightly golden sticks that seem designed for dipping. It also makes biscotti particularly 'good keepers'.

Happily, what works for the corner cafe also works for the home kitchen. Similarly, what works for any occasion, also works for festive times. Biscotti's attributes of being low end labour-wise, flavour adaptable and make it a perfect offering for the for impromptu guests because as long as you have a tin of biscotti around you can impulsively invite anyone for coffee or a spot of tea and know you're prepared.

Four Best Baker's Tips
to start you off:

#1 Butter is not just butter; it's pure gold!

I never take butter for granted because it's always been integral to my baking and never been a bargain ingredient. Butter is both sterling of character and the heart note that holds all baking together. Nowhere is this more evident than in holiday butter cookies. You can call it sweet butter or unsalted butter, but just insist on using *all natural, real butter*. This isn't the time to substitute with anything else (no margarine, no shortening) especially as some recipes are simply butter, sugar and flour. (This all said, if you have some dietary requirements, you can trying substituting cold coconut oil or unsweetened, hard-style margarine)

#2 Vanilla – Only Pure Vanilla Extract – Accept no substitutes

Pure vanilla extract is the core of so much baking, particularly in festive butter-sugar cookies. I use Nielsen Massey Vanilla but you can opt for anything you prefer as long as it's pure and you like the baking results of recipes made with it. Artificial vanilla is totally different from real vanilla and there are varying qualities within that category. Cookies made with artificial vanilla simply don't taste the same and be aware that when you freeze baked cookies made with artificial vanilla; their flavor can go 'off', something the Sara Lee Company discovered decades ago. Even pure or real vanilla can be perfection (as Nielsen Massey is to me) or weaker tasting (depending on the quality and quantity of the vanilla beans used and how it was manufactured). Cookies demand so little really so it pays to invest in the best pure vanilla you can find.

#3 Double Sheeting Pans or "Stack two baking sheets together'

This is one of my best tips and the one that readers of my recipes, my cookbooks and at my website, www. betterbaking.com always comment on. Why do I do this and why is it my number one trick? *Nothing* saves you cookies from uneven baking better than simply using two baking sheets (with parchment paper on the top one). Things bake thoroughly but don't scorch on the outside or edges; the middles of the cookies bake as nicely as the outer edges. Just try this method and you'll thank me with each batch you bake.

#4 Specialty Biscotti Pan

Sometimes it's just easier to use a biscotti pan. These pans (available from Fat Daddio or King Arthur Flour Baker's Catalogue) are perfect for consistently sized and shaped biscotti.

Most biscotti are in fact, baked free-form on a baking sheet. But a pan, especially designed for biscotti, does make things a bit easier. At the least, there's no guesswork in the batter, i.e. loose or a bit firmer, the pan makes remedies errors on either side of the spectrum.

Your Guide to Better Biscotti
Simple Ingredients, Great Extracts, Great Flour!

Traditional biscotti are a matter of few, simple but pure quality ingredients. That said, the number additions ensures that contemporary biscotti knows no limits - no nor shame - in gilding the lily. Since your biscotti are your baking statement and thrive on the personal touch, feel free to add whatever delights you like, creating your own signature biscotti in the process. The thick batter is very accommodating, an affable host to pretty well anything you care to throw in. Plainer biscotti can be gussied up with a slicked on coat of melted chocolate and dusting of chopped pistachios or a sprinkle of confectioners' sugar. To assure baking success, check out these tips towards better biscotti.

Parchment paper makes for less work - no pan greasing - and ensures biscotti won't stick to your baking sheet. Parchment paper, available in gourmet stores, Costco or online can also be used more than once so you can certainly use the same sheets for both the first and second bake.

Heavy, commercial quality baking sheets make life simpler; there's less chance of biscotti burning, ensures even baking, as well as being nice and big which allows biscotti some room to sprawl as the logs bake. For dramatic, extra-long biscotti, use a large commercial baking sheet and make one length of batter - wider and longer than two smaller lengths. The resultant cookies can be some seven to 10 inches in length and really attain that "gourmet" look. Just like my tip for baking better cookies, doubling cookie sheets make for perfect biscotti - baked on top, with no 'surprise' (horrors!) burnt bottoms.

These recipes were tested with unbleached all-purpose flour which is highly recommended for better biscotti. Unbleached all-purpose flour tends to behave exceptionally well in all cookie baking.

Vanilla is the key component for most biscotti, tying in flavours and rounding out the simple tastes. Really upscale biscotti are made with quality, pure vanilla extract - nothing else replicates its natural, subtle bouquet; nothing else contributes quite as much. But after vanilla extract considerations, you also must on insist on other stellar, pure, natural extracts including almond extract and maple etc. Boyijian citrus oils (orange oil, tangerine, lime and lemon) are used in many of my recipes and very often in my biscotti recipes. I would go the extra mile and order some. Otherwise but pure orange and lemon extract are also fine. At all times, use fresh lemon or lime juice.

Baker Tip #1
Cutting Biscotti Made with Nuts

For ultra-thin biscotti that are easily sliced for the second bake, wrap biscotti (whole) overnight and freeze. Next day, using a sharp, serrated knife, slice as thin as you wish and bake the second requisite time to brown. This is also a good tip if you are dealing with biscotti that include whole nuts.

Little Italy's Best Almond Biscotti

Almonds take the lead in this amazingly intense almond biscotti. These are easy but elegant and stuffed with almonds. The top surface has a little sheen or candy-like glaze. Make them big as gifts or little for cookie treat when friends drop by. This is truly my best almond biscotti.

7 ounce (200 g) package of almond paste or marzipan

½ cup unsalted butter, softened

1 ¾ cups sugar

½ cup almonds, finely chopped

4 eggs

1 tablespoon pure vanilla extract

2 teaspoons almond extract

¼ teaspoon salt

1/8 teaspoon cinnamon

½ teaspoon baking soda

1 teaspoon baking powder

4 cups all-purpose flour

1 cup whole blanched almonds

Preheat oven to 350 F. Stack two baking sheets together and line the top one with parchment paper.

Using a hand grater or in a food processor, grate or shred almond paste. In a mixer bowl, cream the almond paste and sugar together (the sugar helps break up the almond paste) then add the butter and blend until mixture is smooth. Stir in the chopped almonds. Then blend in the eggs, vanilla and almond extract and mix well. Fold in salt, cinnamon, baking soda, baking powder, flour and almonds and blend well.

Spoon half of the batter onto each of the baking sheets approximately 9 by 4 inches

Bake 40 minutes until dough is golden and seems dry to the touch. If dough browns too quickly, reduce oven heat to 325 F and bake a little longer to complete.

Remove from oven and cool 20 minutes. Transfer to a board and using a serrated knife on the diagonal, cut slices about 1/2 to 3/4 inch thick.

Reduce oven heat to 300 F. Return cookies to baking sheets. Bake another 35-45 minutes or longer to brown and crisp, turning once, to bake evenly. Cool on wire racks.

Makes 24-36 biscotti, depending on size

Baker's Tip #2
Oven Rack Position

Clementine Cranberry Biscotti

Bake biscotti on the upper third of your oven for even baking without risk of overbrowning the cookie bottoms. If you want to bake two sheets at once, double up the bottom baking sheet (one baking sheet sits inside another) to further insulate this bottom sheet from the direct heat of the oven's bottom element.

Clementine, Cranberry & White Chocolate Biscotti

Make these biscotti once and you'll be legend! This recipe is first baked in a loaf pan like a quick bread. Then the loaf is cut in very thin slices and the slices are baked a second time to crisp the slices. The result is thin wisps of biscotti that are pretty as they are unique. This is a perfect home baked gift. Pack it with a small crate of clementines and attach the recipe.

1 clementine or seedless orange, pureed

½ cup unsalted butter, melted

1 ½ cup sugar

2 eggs

1 teaspoon pure vanilla extract

¼ teaspoon salt

1 ½ teaspoon baking powder

¼ teaspoon cinnamon

2 ¾ cups flour

1 ½ cups dried or chopped frozen cranberries

Finishing Touches

1 cup white chocolate chopped or chips, melted

Preheat oven to 350° F. Spray a 9 by 5 inch loaf pan generously with non-stick cooking spray. Line a baking sheet with parchment paper and place loaf pan on it.

Wash the orange well and cut in quarters (no need to peel orange). Puree the orange in food processor until it reaches the consistency of baby food. Add slices to make ½ cup as required. Remove the puree from the machine.

Without cleaning the work bowl of the food processor, blend the butter, sugar and eggs. Stir in orange puree, then vanilla and mix well.

In a separate bowl, stir together the salt, baking powder, cinnamon, and flour. Fold in wet batter and process to combine. Add in the cranberries.

Transfer batter into prepared loaf pan and smooth out top surface with wet hands. Place loaf pan on baking sheet.

Bake until the top seems set and dry, about 45-55 minutes. If loaf is browning too quickly, reduce heat to 325 and lengthen baking time. Allow to cool 15 minutes before removing from pan and wrap well in foil paper.

Freeze for about 2 hours.

Preheat oven to 325° F. Line two baking sheets with parchment paper. Cut loaf in very thin slices (about 1/8 inch). Place on baking sheets and bake, turning once, about 20-30 minutes, allowing cookies to only lightly brown. Store in an airtight container.

Makes 2-3 dozen biscotti, depending on size

Baker's Tip # 3
Swapping pumpkin for sweet potatoes…

I use sweet potato and canned pumpkin puree interchangeable in recipes such as pie or biscotti. I generally tend to have sweet potatoes always on hand and their flavor in this biscotti, is incomparable. Pureed pumpkin, on the other hand, retains its deep orange colour a bit better.

Sweet Potato Pie Biscotti

This is one of my favourite biscotti recipes and just perfect for Thanksgiving or any holiday but always welcome, no matter what season. These are crisp, spicy and festive, making them a wonderful coffee klatch biscotti or chai-dipping treat. I often coat one side of these with melted white chocolate which I mix with cinnamon or orange oil. They are also wonderful made with roasted sweet pumpkin puree.

¾ cup unsalted butter, melted

1 ½ cups light brown sugar, firmly packed

½ cup white sugar

2 eggs

2 teaspoons pure vanilla extract

¾ cup roasted sweet potato puree (or finely mashed)

2 teaspoons pumpkin pie spice

1 tablespoon cinnamon

¼ teaspoon salt

2 teaspoons baking powder

¼ teaspoon baking soda

4 ½ - 4 ¾ cups all-purpose flour

1 cup chopped walnuts, optional

Finishing Touches

1 cup chopped white chocolate or chips, melted, optional

¼ teaspoon orange oil

½ teaspoon cinnamon

Preheat oven to 350° F. Stack two baking sheets together and line the top one with parchment paper.

In a mixer bowl, blend the butter, brown sugar, white sugar, eggs, vanilla and then blend in the sweet potato puree. Fold in the spices, salt, baking powder, baking soda, most of the flour and the walnuts. Blend to make a stiff dough, adding in more flour as required. Divide dough in two; on the baking sheet, shape each into an 8-10 inch log, about 4-5 inches wide, leaving as much space between them as you can. Bake until the logs are set and dry to the touch about 35 minutes. Remove from the oven and lower the temperature to 325° F.

Cool biscotti 15-20 minutes or until you can easily handle it. Using a sharp, long knife, slice biscotti log into 10-15 slices.

Replace biscotti back on baking sheets and bake a second time to dry and crisp cookies, about 20-30 minutes, turning the cookies once at midway point, to ensure even baking.

Melt the chocolate in a small bowl and stir in the orange oil and/or cinnamon. Using a small metal spatula, coat one side of the biscotti with melted chocolate. Chill to allow chocolate to set.

Makes approximately 30-40 small biscotti

Baker's Tip #4

Frozen Blueberries for Baking

Often recipes (muffins, scones and in this case: biscotti) call for blueberries. When I use blueberries in one of my recipes I often mention the substitution of frozen or semi-frozen berries. Why? Fresh blueberries have a tendency to run or bleed their blue hue into a batter or dough. Sometimes the blue streaks can even turn green (although it all tastes delicious) which, considering we all eat with our eyes, is off-putting. In order to keep the integrity of the look of the finished product, use semi-frozen or frozen fruit. The berries will stay whole and you'll see a nice contrast between the berries and biscotti crumb. Frozen fruit also serves to firm up the batter which is a helpful thing in the case of gloppy biscotti batter.

Blueberries and Cream Biscotti

White chocolate and blueberries marry and make for a country-spirited biscotti that is perfect for a cuppa of English Breakfast tea. Use semi-frozen blueberries and stir gently so they don't break apart and tint the batter blue! If you have any chocolate covered blueberries, you can throw those in too.

1 cup unsalted butter, melted

1 ½ cups sugar

1 tablespoon pure vanilla extract

½ teaspoon lemon oil or extract

¼ teaspoon almond extract

3 eggs

½ teaspoon salt

2 teaspoons baking powder

3 ½ cups all-purpose flour

½ cup white chocolate chunks or chips

½ cup chocolate covered blueberries, optional

1 ½ cups frozen blueberries

Finishing Touches

Coarse sugar

1 cup chopped white chocolate, melted

Preheat oven to 350° F. Stack two baking sheets together and line top one with parchment paper.

In a mixer bowl, blend butter, sugar, vanilla, orange oil, almond extract and eggs together. Blend well about 1 minute.

Fold in salt, baking powder, flour, chocolate, and all types of berries, blending well but taking care not to break berries. If batter seems very loose, add another quarter-cup flour or a few more tablespoons at a time to get a firm or very thick dough.

Pat in two rows on to prepared baking sheet; you should have two lengths of about 3 inches by 8 inches. Dust with sugar (if using). Bake until firm, about 35-40 minutes.

Reduce oven temperature to 325° F. Cool well and then slice on the diagonal, about ½ inch thick, to make long cookies. Place biscotti back on sheet and re-bake to crisp up the cookies, about 15 minutes per side. To finish, cool slightly; using a metal palette knife spread some melted white chocolate on one side of each cookie.

Makes 2 ½ - 3 dozen biscotti, depending on size

Baker's Tip #5

Bake Biscotti in a Biscotti Pan

This is one of my best secrets: great-looking, uniform, easy to cut biscotti, that looks like Starbucks café-style biscotti are not baked free form. Instead, I bake this style of biscotti in a baking pan. You can use a 9 by 13 inch pan, bake the biscotti long and slow and then you have a perfect shaped 'biscotti' loaf to cut. Cut long sticks, and serve or wrap them in cellophane and go into the biscotti business. You can also use this biscotti pan, available via Fat Daddio or King Arthur Baker's Catalogue. Don't pile up the batter too high in these pans because you want sticks of biscotti, not wide slices!

Secret Caramel Chocolate Chip Biscotti

There are many secrets to great biscotti and I share tons of them in all my cookbooks and certainly this biscotti-centric cookbook! But recently, even I found yet another secret that blew the lid open on better biscotti. Bake biscotti in a biscotti pan recommended in the Baker's Tip or even a brownie pan. The pan acts like a biscotti 'girdle', holding the batter in place (no guesswork, no spread) and later on, you're rewarded with huge, professional-looking biscotti which make a fine gift.

Biscotti

1 cup unsalted butter, melted

2 cups sugar

1 tablespoon pure vanilla extract

5 eggs

½ cup finely chopped, toasted almonds

4 cups all-purpose flour

1 package (small or large) caramel pudding (preferably regular, not instant)

2 ½ teaspoons baking powder

¼ teaspoon salt

¾ cup semi-sweet chocolate chips

½ cup butterscotch or Skor Bar chips, optional

1/3 cup chocolate sundae topping

Finishing Touches

Confectioners' sugar

Preheat oven to 350° F. Generously spray a 9 by 13 inch pan with non-stick cooking spray. Then line the pan sides and bottom with parchment paper.

In a mixer bowl, blend the butter and sugar; then blend in the vanilla extract, eggs, and nuts. Fold in the flour, pudding, baking powder, salt and last, the chocolate and caramel chips.

Spoon into the prepared pan, using wet fingers to spread the batter evenly. Drizzle on chocolate syrup on top and swirl it with a butter knife to marbleize. It may all seem a bit messy but it's fine.

Bake until the biscotti are solid to the touch and set, about 55-65 minutes. Cool 15 minutes and then invert onto a cutting surface. Cut in ½ inch slices and place on baking sheet.

Reduce oven temperature to 325° F. Bake biscotti to crisp, 25-30 minutes. Remove and cool well.

Makes 20-24 biscotti, depending on size

Baker's Tip #6
Almond Extra Pro Baker's Tip

My baker's trick? I use a combination of both pure and artificial almond extract for the most intense almond taste possible. One has the subtle, natural almond flavor and the latter (artificial almond extract made from apricot pits) has the bite and lasting flavor that makes almond biscotti really pop.

Chinese Restaurant Almond Cookie Biscotti

I love the crumbly texture, deep yellow colour and intense almond flavor of those almond biscotti, reminiscent of the cookies at Chinese restaurants. Use the smaller amount of yellow food colouring to see how deep a yellow you prefer for your cookies. The combination of natural and artificial almond extract is what gives these biscotti its superlative flavor.

2 ¼ cups sugar

½ cup unsalted butter, melted

½ cup vegetable or corn oil

5 eggs

2 teaspoons pure vanilla extract

2 tablespoons pure almond extract

1 tablespoon artificial almond extract

4 ½ -5 cups all-purpose flour

¼ -½ teaspoon yellow food colouring

½ teaspoon salt

2 ½ teaspoons baking powder

1 cup blanched almonds, optional

Preheat oven to 350° F. Line a baking sheet with parchment paper. Generously spray a 9 by 13 inch rectangular pan with non-stick cooking spray. Place pan on baking sheet.

In a mixer bowl, blend the sugar with the butter and oil. Blend in the eggs and extracts and mix thoroughly. Fold in the flour, food colouring, almonds, salt and baking powder and almonds to make a soft but firm biscotti dough. Pat biscotti dough evenly into the pan

Bake until very solid and set, about 45-60 minutes.

Remove from oven and cool 30 minutes. Turn biscotti out of pan and cut into thick slices and place back on a parchment paper lined pan. Bake in a 325° F oven to re-crisp or further dry out biscotti, about 15 minutes per side.

Makes 1 ½ - 2 dozen biscotti, depending on size

Baker's Tip # 7
Rolling Biscotti in Sugar

Never underestimate sugar, granulated or coarse, as a finishing touch for biscotti, before or after baking. I often dust my biscotti with one or the other before baking, sometimes just pressing in the sugar on the biscotti dough or brushing the biscotti log first with an egg white and then applying the sugar. But after the slice-and-second-bake stage, you can also toss your biscotti (in a bowl or bag filled with sugar) in sugar, along with some spices if you like. It offers extra eye appeal and simply tastes great.

Biscotti versus Mandelbrot

Biscotti is also reminiscent of it European cousin kamishbrot or mandelbrot (which translates to "almond bread"). But mandelbrot is usually oil-based (a concession to Jewish dietary laws) whereas biscotti can be butter-based or oil based or relatively low in fat. Mandelbrot is usually filled with walnuts or almonds and flavored with a bit of cinnamon. Biscotti are usually crispier than mandelbrot due to a longer second baking but either biscotti or mandelbrot, don't bake them until they're dry as sawdust! Better to air on the side of under-baking then over-doing it.

Sugared Cinnamon Walnut Biscotti

This classic and satisfying recipe is one that takes well to variations of spice and additions such as nuts and dried fruit or chocolate. After the biscotti are baked for the second time, you toss them in a sugar and cinnamon mixture which makes them sweet, spicy and totally addictive. These are more like mandelbrot, the iconic cookie from the Jewish kitchen.

1 ½ cups sugar

½ cup canola or vegetable oil

½ cup unsalted butter

4 eggs

1 tablespoon pure vanilla extract

3/8 teaspoon salt

1 tablespoon baking powder

4 cups all-purpose flour

Finishing Touches

1 cup sugar

2 tablespoons cinnamon

Preheat oven to 350° F. Stack two baking sheets together and line the top on with parchment paper.

In a large mixer bowl, blend together the sugar, butter and oil; blend in eggs, and vanilla.

Fold in the salt, baking powder and flour.

Turn mixture onto a lightly covered floured board and shape a log, about 10 by 3 inches, flouring hands if necessary, to avoid sticking. Transfer log on cookie sheet, press down to flatten slightly, and bake until just set, 25-30 minutes.

Remove from oven and let cool 15 minutes. Transfer log to a board, and using long, serrated knife, cut into ½ inch slices. Place cookies back on cookie sheet and bake again at 325° F. to dry and brown slightly (about 15-18 minutes). Turn cookies over once during baking to ensure both sides bake evenly. Cool so that you can handle them.

For cinnamon sugar topping, mix sugar and cinnamon together. Place in a bowl or paper bag. Gently toss biscotti in sugar cinnamon mixture and let excess fall off (in bag or bowl) before assembling on serving platter.

Makes 24-30 biscotti, depending on size

Baker's Tip #8

Toasting the Nuts, Upping the Flavor

Nuts are often featured in biscotti and their crunch and buttery flavor go a long way in making biscotti extra crunchy and inviting. However, if you gently toast or lightly pre-bake the nuts (parchment lined baking sheet, 325° F for 15-20 minutes, with a shuffle during the baking) until lightly browned or a bit golden, the flavor goes through the roof. Sure it's an extra step but it's so worth it. Remember my credo: baking is a series of little things done right.

Maple Pecan Biscotti

Ever since North America's indigenous people discovered the sweet sap of the maple tree, maple syrup has had a shining place in the baker's kitchen. This recipe marries the heritage of pure maple syrup with sweet, toasted pecans. Buttery walnuts would also be perfect in this recipe.

1 cup unsalted butter, melted

1 cup white sugar

¾ cup brown sugar, firmly packed

¼ cup pure maple syrup

1 teaspoon pure maple extract

1 ½ teaspoons pure vanilla extract

3 eggs

4 - 4 /12 cups all-purpose flour

1/3 cup toasted pecans, finely ground

2 teaspoons baking powder

½ teaspoon salt

½ cup chopped toasted pecans

Maple Fondant Glaze

2 cups confectioners' sugar

½ teaspoon maple extract

Whipping cream, as required

Preheat oven to 350° F. Stack two baking sheets together and line the top one with parchment paper. Line a biscotti pan or an 8 by 11 inch rectangular pan (a brownie or pan used for squares is ideal) with parchment paper. Spray the pan (parchment lining as well) with non-stick cooking spray.

In a mixer bowl, hand whisk the butter with the white and brown sugar. Blend in the maple syrup, maple and vanilla extracts, and eggs. Fold in most of the flour, ground pecans, baking powder, salt and chopped pecans to make a thick batter. Spread or pat into pan.

Bake 40 minutes until set and seems firm to the touch; lower temperature to 325° F and bake another 15-20 minutes if biscotti seems not quite baked through; sides seem done but middle may seem 'tender'. Remove and cool 30 minutes and then invert on a platter. Freeze one hour. Preheat oven to 325° F. Cut the biscotti into ½ inch sticks. Place on baking sheet and bake 15 minutes a side, turning once, to crisp biscotti.

Prepare the Maple Fondant by whisking all ingredients together to make a stiff fondant icing or glaze. Smear fondant on one side of each biscotto.

Makes 12-18 biscotti, depending on size

Baker's Tip #9

Lemon Zest in Sugar Disperses More Flavor

Most recipes call for the lemon or orange zest, for that matter, to be tossed in with the flour. However, when you cream the sugar and butter and include the lemon zest at that point, the oils from the zest surrender far more flavor as the citrus oils and butter, along with the sanding effect of the sugar, result in far more pervasive lemon flavor. Biscotti, all baking in fact, are all about great flavor!

Lemon Poppy Seed Biscotti

Sunny Mediterranean flavors in a café-inspired treat. This is the quintessential lemon poppy seed biscotti. Glazing it with fondant offers a boost of eye and taste appeal. Try and use natural lemon oil, such as Boyajian brand.

Biscotti

2 cups sugar

Zest of one lemon, finely grated

Juice of one lemon

½ teaspoon pure lemon oil or pure lemon extract

1 ½ teaspoons pure vanilla extract

½ teaspoon citric acid

5-6 tablespoons poppy seeds

½ cup corn or safflower oil

½ cup unsalted butter, melted

4 eggs

4 ½ cups all-purpose flour

2 ½ teaspoons baking powder

½ teaspoon salt

Lemon Fondant

2 cups confectioners' sugar

Fresh lemon juice, as needed

½ teaspoon pure vanilla extract

¼ teaspoon citric acid, optional

Lemon zest

Preheat oven to 350° F. Stack two baking sheets together and line the top one with parchment paper. Generously spray a 9 by 13 inch pan with non-stick cooking spray and place on the prepared baking sheet.

In a mixer bowl, blend sugar with lemon zest, lemon juice, lemon oil, vanilla extract, citric acid and poppy seeds. Add in oil, butter and blend one minute and then add in eggs and blend well. Fold in flour, baking powder and salt and blend well, on slow speed of mixer 1-2 minutes. Spread out in two or one large log into the pan. Brush with egg wash and sugar.

Bake 55-65 minutes until set. Cool about 20 minutes and then cut into ¾ -1 inch sticks. In a 325° F oven, bake the biscotti 15 minutes a side to dry out. Cool well. If using Lemon Fondant, mix ingredients together to make a soft glaze. Spread over each biscotti stick, dust on poppy seeds and lemon zest. Allow fondant to set.

Makes 14-24 biscotti, depending on size

Baker's Tip # 10

Don't Overbake Your Biscotti

Do not overbake your biscotti. Biscotti continues to crisp as it cools. Take biscotti out of the oven as soon as it appears lightly colored and dry to the touch. Biscotti does most of its crisping in the oven but it certainly does crisp up more as it cools so don't overbake. As it cools, it will achieve its final crunchy texture.

Chocolate Chunk Tollhouse Biscotti

Blockbuster sticks of crisp, buttery biscotti, fragrant with butter, vanilla, and graced and shot through with Swiss chocolate. You can glaze these or just toss in sugar as per the recipe.

1 cup unsalted butter, melted

1 ½ cups white sugar

½ cup brown sugar, firmly packed

5 eggs

1 tablespoon pure vanilla extract

1/8 teaspoon pure almond extract

4 ½ - 5 cups all-purpose flour

2 ½ teaspoons baking powder

½ teaspoon salt

1 cup semi-sweet chocolate chips or chopped chocolate bar

1 cup milk chocolate chips or chopped chocolate bar

Sugar Toss

1 ½ cups sugar

¼ teaspoon cinnamon

1 teaspoon vanilla powder, optional

¼ cup cocoa

Finishing Touches

1 cup confectioners' sugar

1-2 tablespoons water or cream

1 teaspoon pure vanilla extract or ½ teaspoon orange oil

Preheat oven to 350° F. Stack two baking sheets together and line the top one with parchment paper.

In a mixer bowl, blend the butter with the sugar; then add in the eggs, vanilla and almond extracts and blend well. Fold in the flour, baking powder and salt and blend somewhat and then add in the chocolate chips. Let batter stand 5-10 minutes.

Using wet hands, spread batter out onto baking sheet and shape into a log of 12 inches or so long, and 4-5 inches wide. Pat to shape into a neat shape.

Bake until set up and done, about 45-60 minutes. If biscotti starts to brown but still does not appear set, reduce oven temperature to 325° F and bake until set.

Cool well, and then slice into diagonal sticks, about ¾ inch wide. Place back on baking sheet (you will probably need two parchment lined baking sheets to hold all the biscotti in one layer and not squish them)|. Bake at 325° F 20-30 minutes, turning once, to lightly brown and crisp biscotti. For Sugar Toss, mix sugar, cinnamon, vanilla and cocoa in a medium bowl. Toss baked, cooled biscotti in sugar toss. (They are ready to serve)

If using the Glaze, in a small bowl, mix the sugar, water or cream and vanilla to make a soft glaze. Using a small metal palette knife, smear on one side of each biscotti stick and let set.

Makes 20-32 biscotti, depending on size

Baker's Tip #11
Softer Biscotti Batter When Layering

When you're creating a biscotti of two layers, such as in the Raspberry Cheesecake Biscotti, it's alright to have a slightly softer batter to spread on top as seen here. The soft batter will spread out and cover the middle section.

Raspberry Cheesecake Biscotti

Who doesn't like raspberry cheesecake, even when it's in a biscotti rendition? Make these biscotti the traditional way or do them pan-style for a polished café-bistro style look.

Biscotti Batter

1 cup unsalted butter, softened

1 ¾ cup sugar

4 eggs

2 ½ teaspoons pure vanilla extract

3 ¼ cups all-purpose flour

2 ½ teaspoons baking powder

¼ teaspoon salt

1 cup raspberry preserves

2 tablespoons raspberry liqueur or raspberry eau de vie

Cream Cheese Fondant

2 ½ cups confectioners' sugar

4 tablespoons cream cheese, softened

1 teaspoon pure vanilla extract

1 teaspoon lemon juice

Water or light cream, as required

Preheat oven to 350° F. Stack two large baking sheets together and line the top one with parchment paper. For pan style biscotti, generously spray a 9 by 10 inch pan with non-stick cookie spray and place on baking sheets.

In a mixer bowl, blend the butter and sugar until well-combined. Add in the eggs, vanilla, flour, baking powder and salt; blend to make a stiff batter, adding in more flour if mixture seems too wet or gloppy (it should be quite thick).

Form half the biscotti batter on the baking sheet in a 9-10 inch oblong. In a small bowl mix the raspberry jam with the raspberry liqueur. Spread half the raspberry jam on the biscotti batter. Then pat or drop chunks of the remaining batter on top. Using floured or wet hands, pat down the length somewhat. This is a soft batter and it will spread. If using the pan method, spread half the batter in the pan. Top with the remaining jam and batter (spread in chunks as best you can).

Bake 30 minutes and then reduce the temperature to 325° F for another 35-40 minutes until biscotti are set and lightly brown all over. Remove biscotti from the oven. Cool one hour (or freeze them) and then cut into sticks, about ½ inch thick. Replace on baking sheet and bake in a 325° F oven to crisp biscotti, about 25-35 minutes.

For the Cream Cheese Fondant, in a medium bowl, blend confectioners' sugar, cream cheese, vanilla extract, lemon juice and water or cream to make soft glaze.

Smear on cooled biscotti sticks, on top surface and let set.

Makes 12-18 biscotti, depending on size

Baker's Tip # 12
Chocolate Glazing

All biscotti can be further gilded by finishing with a chocolate glaze. To glaze biscotti, melt whatever chocolate you're using (white, dark, milk) gently (a double-boiler is best) and keep just warm. Use a flat, small icing knife, spread melted chocolate on one side of each cookie. Cool on rack 2-4 hours until thoroughly dry. You can also freeze them but the gloss of the chocolate will dull. Alternatively, simply dip one end of each biscotti in the melted chocolate, or even double dip, i.e. dip once into the dark chocolate and let set. Then dip a second, more "shallow" dip into the white chocolate or vice versa.

Double Chocolate Biscotti

Some people can never get enough chocolate which makes this a go-to biscotti for the chocaholic in your circle.

¾ cup unsalted butter, melted, still warm

½ cup cocoa, measured then sifted

1 ½ cups sugar

4 eggs

3 tablespoons whipping cream

2 teaspoons pure vanilla extract

¼ teaspoon salt

2 teaspoons baking powder

¼ teaspoon baking soda

3-4 cups all-purpose flour

½ cup semi-sweet chocolate in coarse chunks

½ cup milk chocolate chips

½ cup white chocolate chips

Finishing Touches

¾ cup white chocolate, melted

Preheat oven to 350° F. Stack two baking sheets together and line the top one with parchment paper.

In a mixer bowl, blend the melted butter with the cocoa. Blend in sugar, eggs, vanilla and whipping cream.

In a separate bowl, blend salt, baking powder, baking soda and flour. Stir into wet ingredients and then fold in all the chocolate. The mixture should be very thick. With wet hands, spread out onto prepared baking sheets to about 8 by 4 inches.

Bake until top seems set, around 30-40 minutes. Let cool 15 minutes. Transfer to a board and cut, on the diagonal, into wedges ½ to ¾ inch thick. Reduce oven temperature to 325° F. Transfer cookies to baking sheets and return to oven. Bake 15-20 minutes to dry, turning once midway to brown evenly. Since cookies are dark, it is difficult to see when they are done. They should seem almost dry to the touch when ready but keep an eye on them

For the coating, melt the white chocolate slowly You can spread or drizzle on melted white chocolate on one side of these baked cookies for a more gourmet look.

Makes 18-24 biscotti, depending on size

Baker's Tip #13
California Apricots for Baking

It's getting a bit more difficult to find vibrant, flavorful California apricots to bake with. But nothing beats their flavor! I order mine from Bella Viva Orchards. They have so many types of California apricots, not to mention other outstanding dried fruit for all your baking.

Apricot Sunrise Biscotti

Some folks swoon for chocolate; I swoon for apricots. This biscotti features Californian dried apricots and is graced with a dash of apricot liqueur (peach schnapps or orange juice are good swaps)). These biscotti are sweet, tart, and pretty as a picture. Baking with liqueurs is always interesting and this method of dipping the baked biscotti into juice or wine and then sugar and re-baking, is one I favour. It looks and taste amazing!

½ cup unsalted butter, melted

1 ½ cups sugar

2 eggs

1 ½ teaspoons pure vanilla extract

½ teaspoon orange oil or extract

½ cup peach schnapps, apricot liqueur or nectar

Zest of one orange, finely minced

1 tablespoon baking powder

¼ teaspoon salt

3-4 cups all-purpose flour

4 cups diced dried California apricots

½ cup minced yellow raisins

Finishing Touches

1 cup apricot liqueur, peach schnapps or orange juice

1 cup sugar

Preheat the oven to 350° F. Stack two baking sheets together and line the top one with parchment paper.

In a mixer bowl, cream the butter and sugar; add eggs, vanilla and orange oil and blend well. Fold in remaining ingredients and blend for one minute to make a thick, pasty mixture. Spread mixture out on the baking sheet in one large or two medium logs of batter, about 4-5 inches wide and 8 to 10 inches long. Bake until set, about 35-45 minutes.

Remove from oven and cool about 20 minutes before cutting into diagonal lengths, about ½ - ¾ inch wide. Dip each cookie, one side only, in juice or liqueur and then press into sugar.

Place sugar side down on baking sheet.

Lower oven temperature to 325° F. Bake to crisp biscotti, about 20-30 minutes. Remove from oven and cool well.

Makes 18-24 biscotti, depending on size

Bonus Recipes with Purchase!

Free 4-Months Access! Betterbaking.com

Please join me on this journey as we embark on another Baker's Dozen Recipe book. I wish you great success as you bake each and every one of these special recipes. Don't forget my gift to you with your purchase! Just email me at www.betterbaking.com with an electronic proof of purchase to obtain your four bonus free month subscription to Betterbaking.com. You'll enjoy access to over 2500 more of my recipes online at my site.

Acknowledgements

Editorial Team

Senior Editors

Wendy Berman, Jan Hirsch, Phyllisa Goldenberg, Sherri Seidmon

Recipe Testers

The following people graciously volunteered their time, energy, and ingredients in testing the recipes. I can't thank them enough. They ensured my recipes are as accurate and as exacting as possible so that you can have the same success when you bake these delicious recipes.

Karyl Barron	Naomi Lansky
Wendy Berman	Marla Marcus
Uli Cotter	Lee Picard
Wendy Christie	Sherri Seidmon
Diane DiVittorio	Sharon Schach
Laurie Drazner	Robin Schatz
Thea Finklestein	Bonnie Schultz
Joyce Leitman	Caryn Stellman
Janet Gardner	Linda Sterling
Susan Hatch	Amy Stromberg
Jan Hirsch	Vanessa Roland
Denise Kitchel	Lois Urdowitz
Shelley Koebel	Carol Weinstein
Phyllisa Goldenberg	Karen Schwartz Wirima

Other Cookbooks by Marcy Goldman

If you've enjoyed this Baker's Dozen cookbook, please check out my other titles, available in print and e-books from Amazon, Kindle, Indigo, Barnes and Noble or wherever you purchase your books.

Each title is quite distinct in its recipe style and I've packed each and every book with great baking information and product sources so you can bake you very best!

Warm wishes and happy baking,

Marcy Goldman

Author, Master Baker

www.BetterBaking.com

BESTSELLING AUTHOR OF TREASURY OF JEWISH HOLIDAY BAKING

THE BAKER'S DOZEN
Cookbook Series Volume 2

BEST BISCOTTI

Marcy Goldman

Author of Treasury of Jewish Holiday Baking
Host, Betterbaking.com

THE BAKER'S DOZEN
Cookbook Series Volume 1

BEST HOLIDAY COOKIES

Marcy Goldman

Author, A Passion for Baking
When Bakers Cook, and Host, Betterbaking.com

The Baker's Four Seasons

BAKING BY THE SEASON, HARVEST AND OCCASION

Marcy Goldman

Author of *A Passion for Baking*, *When Bakers Cook*, and host of *Betterbaking.com*

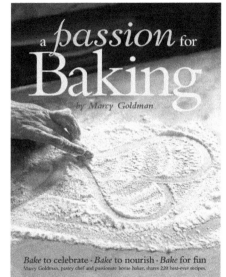

a *passion* for
Baking
by Marcy Goldman

Bake to celebrate · *Bake* to nourish · *Bake* for fun
Marcy Goldman, pastry chef and passionate home baker, shares 220 best-ever recipes.

the *new* best of
BETTER BAKING
.com

More than 200 classic recipes
from the beloved baker's website

With 30 new and exciting recipes

MARCY GOLDMAN

A Treasury of
JEWISH HOLIDAY BAKING

The 10th Anniversary Edition
Marcy Goldman

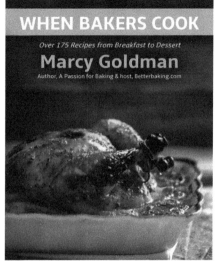

WHEN BAKERS COOK

Over 175 Recipes from Breakfast to Dessert
Marcy Goldman
Author, A Passion for Baking & host, Betterbaking.com

Baker Boulanger
BETTER BAKING.COM
Marcy Goldman, Master Baker
A baker's heart
is
Est. 1997